I MISS THE ZOO
AND OTHER POETRY SELECTIONS

JOSEPH ARTHUR

EM PRESS

Dedicated
to
so and so
something nice about
that person

Collecting poems for a book
I'm happiest
When writing poems
Or playing with melodies
Or painting
But mostly poetry
Feels like the essence
I see myself old
And writing
When all the chaos has faded
I'll come back to words
And let them save me
And invent me
Into old age
And then I'll let them
Introduce me
To the stars.

These poems are collected
And so to me they are like trapped
Animals that never found a home
Their potential for me stops here
But for you they can live
And push and maybe even inspire
They are yours now
For whatever that's worth
More yours than mine
Mine is the next one
The one that's not here yet
These are like ghosts of lost times
Gathered here sparking in
collections of dust
A love letter to the future
To death
To love itself
Walking away from belief
And into the sky of not knowing

Enjoy every second you get
For you were gone before
you came
And I was right there with you

Cover art and book design by Derek Broad and
Sinbad Richardson at the Cardboard Box Project
Back page photo Danny Clinch
Copy edited by Newsha Mostafavi

ISBN: 978-0-9850946-3-8

Printed in the United States of America for EM Press, LLC.
First printing, 2013

EM Press
24041 S. Navajo Dr.
Channahon, IL 60410
www.em-press.com

CONTENTS

TRAVEL AS EQUALS (OR NOT AT ALL)

In the dark of graveyard chatter
In the light of freedom's call
In the heat of any matter
We travel as equals or not at all
Bloom disgust and class divide
I saw it written on the wall
The only way we can survive
We travel as equals or not at all
You can't be in greater comfort
As my pain prevents your fall
The truth will come and tell us, brother
We travel as equals or not at all

And when we get to where we're going
Past the divide, past the stall
Past the wind that's always blowing
Travel as equals or not at all
You might have a greater income
Or you might be dumb and dull
But either way I won't leave you
Travel as equals or not at all

So help me, too, in my slumber
If I'm blind in madness hall
If I'm deaf amongst the thunder
Travel as equals or not at all
Lift the way, forget the ransom
Free the chain and kick the ball
Let our love take us higher
Travel as equals or not at all

And down the road
And through the sky
And on the tracks
Hear the gull
Fly above us
Without worry
Travel as equals or not at all
I hope your road takes you homeward
And may you always outrun the law
If I'm with you, we will always
Travel as equals or not at all

Yes, if I'm with you
We will always
Travel as equals or not at all

Yes, if I'm with you
We will always
Travel as equals or not at all

THE RARE ONES

Sweetness
Is an underrated virtue
It might be
The very best
Kindness
A gentle soul

The Empire State Building is green with envy tonight
I see it from Jersey
I think that great landmark
Might have an idea
Something's going on over here

Sometimes
People speak with poison
They try sometimes
To take you with their pain
Just remember
Don't believe them
Just remember
It's their pain
Not your own
Just remember
It's their fear
Not yours

Sweetness
Is an underrated virtue
I often think of that Neil Young song
Heart of Gold
Where he sings something like,
"Been searchin' for a heart of gold
And I'm growin' old"
I think I know what he means
Not that I haven't found golden hearts along the way
It's more that now
I appreciate the rarity of it

Sweetness
The underrated virtue
When someone's kind
When they don't stab you with barbed language
And then deny your right to feel any pain

Those are the rare ones

SPIRITUAL MEXICO

This is the shape of my dream
Bloody and cold
This moment of time fragmented
Fermented and old
But still in the prime of life
Electric circuit-shaped
Cut and fresh
Like Tron through the light in Manhattan
Computer-age dazzled
Hard wind already blowing
Hard rain already coming
This is the shape of my dream
Tattoo New York
City kid poor
Richer than before
Artist on the loose
On the verge of the real letting go
On the verge of spiritual Mexico

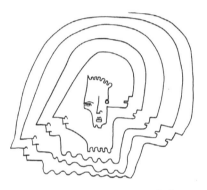

Each day asks only that you find
your way through the muck and back
to the source to plug yourself into the
infinite and spin like a top.

THREW THE KEYS ON MY WINDSHIELD
AND CRACKED IT

Threw the keys on my windshield and cracked it
Now we drive with lines in our eyes between states of mind
And cities of refusal
I used to know more
I used to believe in time
I used to think I was a person
I used to have a name
Now I'm a stucco wall
With flesh pinned against it
And speckles of blood spinning like planets around a mind or
a sun
Which heats this universe with the fire of dreams
Stoked in the center by imagination and criminal character

The spirit has come from flesh
The flesh falls away
The spirit soars
It breaks apart
It becomes undone
It goes beyond
Think of your body like a cocoon
Think of your spirit like a butterfly
The flesh will fall
You will be free
This world is a ghetto
My windshield is cracked
Words are no good except in poetry
That's why nobody likes poetry
Especially good poetry
Nobody wants to be woken from their slumber

I am a plunger next to your toilet
Your soul is a toilet
I'm a soul plunger
Morality is just God trying to make your trip here easier on you
Nothing more
It falls away with your flesh
You want true rebellion?
You want true punk rock n' roll?
Then be sober and moral
And you will fly in the face of everyone and everything
You will save the whole world
You will make the ghetto a palace
A kingdom of light
And you will enjoy bliss
And not some soft angelic version
But a badass fun as fuck
Rock n' roll bliss

My windshield is cracked and I'm on my way to Philly
I am the cracked messiah
I am Boogie Christ
Don't trust me
I don't give a fuck
This is the ghetto
This is a smoke stack of cancer and confusion
The body is a shell for the butterfly
This world is training for the next

But you will not be you
You will be free
And the sewer that is your ego will break apart like links of an
old chain
And you will be happy to see it go

You will be happy to see you go
But that said
This world is an opportunity to fund and find bliss
It can be done
It's really here if you want it
But don't take it too seriously
Just be moral and make it easy on yourself
And beat the heart of true rebellion

Burn white hot
And hotter than the sun
At the center of the sun
Be the liberated seer of the apocalypse
Save everybody's ass and then die with a smile on your face
As you blow up like an atom bomb
Into God

PROPELLED BY LOVE

Propelled by love-
As we march through our routines
Desensitized
Marching through chaos
Propelled by the love of others
Propelled by love
Past death and oblivion
Propelled by love
Straight to the pulse of life
Waking up to itself
Inside of us
The consciousness of a million galaxies
All floating
In our three pound universe
Orbiting
A thousand suns
Across centuries
Across all of time,
Propelled by love's past protection,
Through nudity
As the spirit wanders into itself
Realized

THE CIRCUS BLEW THROUGH ME

The circus blew through me
Magic people of blue light radiance
Let go of all fear
And set their angles toward the sun
Inside out we wandered about the moon
And finally fell to the earth
Whole and complete
Awake and exhausted
We fell asleep
And so our dreams reinterpreted for us
The events that fell through mud slides
Of sonic glories as they sank into the past
Along with the seeds of their inspiration
Where they can grow in people's minds and memories
Into forests of insight
Magic people of blue radiance
All living in LA
Which has earned and earns its reputation as a strange place
A place at the beginning and end of time
A place where new dreamers meet the ones
whose dreams have died
Over coffee and elevator music and plastic puppets of the apocalypse
Dangle temptation and illicit versions of a false freedom
Which swings death into a zombie dance in the minds of children
Across this world and the next
Yet still
The magic people of blue radiance
They came to sing my song
And help lift me into white light
Where my sins were washed away on the shores of freedom
And I became a thousand birds flying at dusk out of the madness of
the city

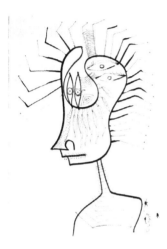

I will neither lose nor check back in.
I will neither find nor give blood for
I am full of feathers and stones and
fire ants and broken homes.

FOR YOUR CONSIDERATION

For your consideration
We all had movie reels
Performances we had done
We wanted each other to watch
To judge
To approve
To say we had been great
To say there was nobody better
To give the love and respect
So that our own attack dogs
Which by now had grown tired and insane
Which by now had turned around
And been nipping at us
Growling at us
And even from time to time lunging at us
Would somehow be calmed
Would somehow
Be placated
As if thrown a toy or a steak
Or the head of a forgotten dictator
Which somehow still managed to speak to them
Pleading "back off"
Right before they chewed off his nose
The reels said
"For your consideration"
But they might as well have said
For my salvation
We didn't want to be abandoned at the well
Or refused at that velvet rope
But the truth is
So many of us were

And so we walked like zombies up and down Hollywood
Boulevard
The stars beneath our feet
Most of them long ago in their grave
Most of them had flown across romantic night skies
A long time ago
In the past
Most of them liberated from ideas
Of even being a star in the street
Locked in concrete
With vagrants dragging their feet
Across the face of their memory
Most of them
Liberated from show reels
And our consideration
And if they could somehow speak to us now
I bet they would say
Throw your show reels
Under the wheels of the next car that flies right by
And remember you are all these stars illuminated
On this desolate street
About to fly out of the concrete
And soar across the night sky of now
And fall into the eyes
Of a child
Dreaming for your consideration

It sends you shooting through darkness
with a backwards heart. Afraid. But
this life is a dream and no matter what
they say, you are infinite.

SOME DAYS

Some days you do anything to stay in
Don't get dressed 'til four PM
And wander around your kitchen
Like a Times Square hobo
Dig through your own garbage
See your past flash before you, like an old home movie
As you look at yourself in the bathroom mirror
Brushing your teeth
Pop out your glass eyeballs and soak 'em in gasoline
So your vision can catch fire
So you can see into the future
Unscrew your ears and flip 'em
So you hear everything backwards
Take your nose off and put it in a bowl of flowers and let it sit
there over night
Enhancing your perspective to the sweetness of the world
Change your wig a thousand times 'til your hair is just perfect
And flip your mouth upside down so it's not as easy to lie
And then light your eyes up and pop them blazing back into your
skull
Then cry the fires out
And walk down the street
A rotten corpse
Smelling the sweetness of it all
As you see a future in flames
Where upside down voices tell you they love you backwards
And when you say hello
You mean goodbye
And when you say
How are you?
You mean

Why am I here?
And all the answers are witchy and mysterious
And your glass eyes see
How beyond your death
You will live all this again
In the dreams of your children
And their children's children
And you will recognize yourself in the folly of it all
A ghost attached to nothing
As you were in life
So shall you be in death
A master of lowliness
A serpent of loneliness
A king of untouched grace
Put together by artificial parts
In the heart of nature
A true believer
Who doesn't try to make anything beyond what it is

INSIDE OF ME THERE IS A BEGGING BOWL

Inside of me there is a begging bowl
Empty as the sun pretends to be
And as I drop to whisper in its hole
A random spirit comes to visit me
And you will say goodnight to every man
The ones you touch as if with a phantom hand

Upon new skin and desert tides of love
You have begun to play with death again
Lost beneath your fiction a phantom glove
Will you come alive as the light within?
And we can weep but not from sadness now
And in your field for dreams, the endless plow

To escape this body and mortal place
To ascend beyond the reach of your will
To wear for now, an angel's loving face
To be of earth without the need to kill
And so you paint your name on twilight skies
And so you transcend the realm of goodbyes

And all is forgiven for a moment
And in your charge, the will of God is found
And all is enlivened and silent
And in your hope, the hope of man unbound
And now you've gone beyond the reach of life
To liberate your heart without a knife

NOTHING IS GLAMOROUS

Nothing is glamorous
My day is deranged from the start
Some jazz band plays in the corner
From some distant time
Their sound still reaching my mind
As I stare out the window into the Brooklyn sun
Burning the crowd
As they walk
Stand still
And run
Like a sax solo
People float in and out of different modes
Clash into each other
Hit a sharp turn
Just miss each other
Reach a flat
Then go on their merry way
Resolve the chaos
The train rolls by
Magically overhead
Like all the things I should be doing but don't want to
Flowing into the city

A song comes to mind

Love will save us all
But seems in short supply
The phantoms play their jazz
To the strangers walking by
Love will save us all

But is like a slight of hand
If the savior comes at all
He will live amongst the damned

Love will save us all
But love pollutes like dope
A little fills your heart
With the thunder cloud of hope

It threatens to come down
And soon someday it will
As the thing that gives you life
Comes in now for the kill

Love will save us all
But we must be its spark
As we hide out from ourselves
In the comfort of the dark

Nothing is glamorous
My day is deranged from the start
Some jazz band plays in the corner
From some distant time
Their sound still reaching my mind
As I stare out the window into the Brooklyn sun

It will always be an incomplete
education and it will always be a voided
celebration so say goodbye at the sta-
tion and get on the train.

I WOKE UP AT 4:30

I woke up at 4:30
How are you?
I've split up with reality
I like the zoo
Let's go live
In the monkey cage
Let's just hibernate
Through the winter
Of our dusk
Twisted up like fate
I wish we could
Talk some more
But your words
Truly splinter
And tiny shards
Like wild cards
Change for me the center
And tiny shards
Like wild cards
Get stuck inside my brain
And on the tracks
I move through fields
On a burning train
Horses follow
And homeward doves
Chased by crows at night
I look to you
But get struck blind
By the gift of second sight
Let's collect our misery
In houses made of bones

And cover them with hide and skin
And call it all our own
And let's pretend that we are them
The ones still throwing stone
At the wall
That's never there
We ricochet alone
Bloom disgust and highway greed
Survival is a trick
You turn and burn and look away
From the children who are sick
Is God a loon?
What will become
Of this story as it lives
With feelings real
And souls that steal
What bodies can't forgive
The elders say
They've had enough
They're ready to move on
But they want to see
The children
Who will dream and carry on
Through the maze of suffering
Through the rooms of loss
If you make it
Through the void
A hand, a coin, you toss
Heads you win
Tails you lose
The world is made of chance
God is mad
And for our food

He wants to watch us dance
Yes, God is mad
And for our food
He wants for us to dance

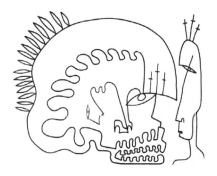

What's with the stars? Things in focus.
Guided of course, but you don't always
know, and sometimes it seems impossible.
It's not.

THE BALLAD OF BOOGIE CHRIST

Christ would wear cowboy boots
Christ would have sex
Christ would eat pizza
And cut Blackjack decks
Christ would be sober
But Christ would be fun
Christ would get over
On those trying to run
Christ would love hip hop
Metal and soul
Christ would bring chaos
The breath of control
Christ would be rocking
Christ would be free
He'd say there's no difference
Between you and me
This is the ballad of Boogie Christ
Toss my salad
Feed me your rice

Christ baked potatoes
Christ chewing gum
Christ without pathos
Saying "yum yum"
Christ in the middle
Like the monkey with balls
Christ picking up
When euphoria calls
Hello, dear father
Hello there, my son

How have you been?
Well, I gotta run
Ok I love you
See you real soon
Maybe September
Maybe next June

This is the ballad of Boogie Christ
Toss my salad
And throw wedding rice

Christ would be careful
Christ would be brave
But Christ, he would never
Be anyone's slave
Christ is here now
Christ is beyond
Christ would watch Rocky
And On Golden Pond
Christ would relax
And Christ would get mad
Christ would help answer
If judgment is bad
Well, no and then yes
Well, yes and then no
Nothing is easy
But it's simple to glow
Just walk away
From fear and deceit
Never surrender
But never compete
Cheer for your brother
Your rival, your friend

Help their survival
To beat you again

This is the ballad of Boogie Christ
Toss my salad
And feed me some rice

Give and give freely
All that you can
And help show the worried
What it is to be man
Christ would be handsome
Christ would be gross
Christ would buy butter
And make you some toast
Christ would be savage
But Christ would be true
He'd say if you want him
Then look inside you
Yes, Christ would be savage
But Christ would be true
He'd say if you want him
Then just look in you

This is the ballad of Boogie Christ
Toss my salad
Throw wedding rice

This is the ballad of Boogie Christ
Toss my salad
Throw wedding rice

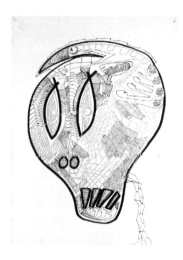

Drugs or enlightenment?
No fear or insanity?
He said he met a retired ball
player and they were gonna make
a killing in real estate.

OMENS

There are many omens in the city
Dead rats frozen in motion and squashed under a thousand tires
A one-legged pigeon
A Mexican eating sushi on a corner wearing a cowboy hat
A hooker with two heads and a calendar tacked to her back
Black cats are the least of it
I gladly walk under ladders
And step on cracks
'Cause when you see a three-legged dog
Playing chess with a thundercloud
Then you really must be careful
The city full of omens
People speaking with eyes
And nature communicating
Through various signs of death looming everywhere
There is no one but you
And the vast eternity of nothingness and space
Nothing to hold you
To this place
So the omens
Come calling
And the dark wind
Howling your name
As you ride over squirrels
Already smashed by the need to be home

THE BIG SLEEP

There comes a time
When you're ready
To reckon
Or face yourself
Or try again
To be whole
When you've been a hole
And everything
Gets sucked inside
And you realize
It'll just go on
'Til you find
Something quiet
Inside yourself
Like a voice of your essence
Showing you again
A way to love
A way to forgive
And a way to believe
That freedom
Is something earned
But not beyond you

Then everything is simple again
And somewhat clear
Whoever you've been
Wherever you've been
Don't really matter now
For now
You just woke up

Out of a big sleep
And the past is like all the dreams that faded from your memory
And you do something simple
Like walk down the street
And the snow is melting on the ground
And the last sun
Blasts in an incredible sky
And when you walk into its beam
You ask the creator to heal you
To let the light wash over you
And make you new
And then a bum asks for some change
And you reach for it
For it strikes you as an answer to your prayer
He asks what your hat is made of
And you tell him as you give him a buck
And then you keep walking
As a smile miraculously creeps across your face
And you realize
The day is different now

Riding the subway home. Listening
to Lou, "Coney Island Baby." I see a
girl on the nod. I want to tell her it'll
be all right but maybe it won't.

I HAD WANDERED THROUGH THE SNOW

I had wandered through the snow
Everyone had turned against me
And then I became invisible
I wandered on
But then I was massive
Then I was a mountain
No one could climb
And so I was alone with the sky
And I saw you run like an ant around my grave
And I saw you forget me so fast as it rained
As I rained
I was a cloud
I just sat there in the sky
Until I started to fall
Calling you with each drop on your face
Trying to be your tears
I ran down your cheek
And still I was surprised how easily you wiped me away
I practiced yoga
Breathing backwards
And then I was a bird
It was old age
I flew alone
In the burgundy sun
The grey sky swallowed me whole and then I was a baby again
In the arms of the new mother
Sucking for life
Nourishment
If only to survive for dreams
Before my voice was born
Another came to me and said

You are a machine for dreams
A body to house my imagination
And you are eyes
To see the beauty I create and the love I condemn
And then I was a rose
Wilting on the edge of a toxic moon
Breaking open like an egg for ghost

I COME DOWN

I come down
And I don't know
Who I was
Or
Where I was
I come down
And the tattoos
Of distant avenues
Litter my skin
Like the junk of fallen thieves
I come down
And I have myself
Been crucified
Against myself
Once again
On my knees
I come down
And belief is a residue of everything seeming man-made and
none too pure
I come down
A cadaver
Hanging there in thin air
Like so many forgotten sons
Or bugs who just float through thin air
I come down
And don't know
Who I thought I was
Writing and saying things
That resemble
A madman
A saint

A trickster
A megalomaniac
A poet
And even
A reasonable human being
I come down
And all of the voices which once ripped through infinity's sky
Like the screen on a television set only to my eye
Giving me lieutenants and sergeants of war like angels who
beg me and have fallen before to tell me their secret
To write through the flower with the power of mercy
Still locked from the door
I come down
And there is no longer an adequate version of me
Maybe he disappeared when I gave into moments of useless bravado
myself to the puppets like pearls before swine
Maybe I just slipped away and left myself in zombie skin to walk
amongst the dead merely a shadow of who I've been
I come down
And there is no justice on streets like these where the only thing
that makes a difference is the thickness of your stack
or the size of your blade
Where woman are merely objects to protect or to be stolen
and leave to crumble further into your own vacancy
I come down
And I see through the eyes seeing through me
I see those dark eyes and I notice them notice the weapon I flash
so they know not to try it on me
I come down
And my anger is pure and though my strength with angels has
devolved my strength on the street is all encompassing
and knows no bounds
For purely animal attack

Survival we built not the same
Me
Warrior heart
All ache and pain
To bring it
Back to them
When I come down
They keep me down
And down I'm home
With the rats scurrying along pipes of no chance
Where blood and points mix up looking to stick and shoot
into the final heart of empty salvation
I come down
Forget your heroes here
We live
Hand to mouth
And what you did then
Hardly matters
Each man has a back
And only one back to watch
I come down

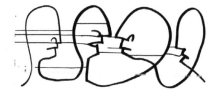

When I drink, drink with me. When
I beg, please answer. Our dreams are
never as dark as we think they are,
and our lives are children songs.

YOUR MESSAGE HAD NO CONTENT

Your message had no content
Your truth is a deflated soccer ball
being kicked in a dust bowl by a leper
Your dream is a minnow going down a toilet bowl
Spinning forever waiting for the final flush
You are done with this life
Not believing in much but material possession
And your collection of souls
You are a king of snakes
A deception fucking the desert 'til it's green
and filled with horrendous life
Your message has no content
And you have no will of your own
Guided by impulse and unconscious will to protect
and destroy what you destroy and protect
Are you still using the excuse of your childhood?
That child is gone
He is a ghost or even a ghoul
He is a voice in your vampire head
He is insanity playing tennis with a broken racket
Against a wall that's falling down
Your message has been deleted from the server
Along with your photographs and phone numbers
I couldn't find you if I wanted
But in any event you are always here telling me
What to do
And how I've failed and biting my head off
After kissing my cheek
And spitting it like a seed into the eye of a hurricane
Your message has erased my mind
As I sit in a dressing room surrounded by mirrors and light bulbs
Unable to see the reflection of anyone

DAMN. I FORGOT TO WRITE A POEM

Damn. I forgot to write a poem
I let you put a diamond in my nose
I let you wander past food stamps into tattoos and goldmines
I let us eat flapjacks with grits at The Majestic
I let you let me spank you spank me
I let us rub the surface off a hundred lotto tickets to win two
dollars back and rub those to void
I let us buy dream guitars, which fold distortion like angels
kissing the ears of the deaf and the eyes of the blind
I let you free me by surrendering elastic handcuffs
After you said, choke me but be careful
And we never had a safety word
And we never practiced yoga but instead let our bellies grow out
around Ponce de Leon
And I really didn't remember enough of those old streets
Enough at least to forget them
And you even let me grow my beard
And eat vegetarian soul food and play long guitar solos
And feel love
For everyone all the time
And be awake
And be grateful
And have folks that love me
And surrender to your will
And do so with gratitude and happily
And you let me ride next to an easel and you let paint
fall from the roof
Of the rust machine and paint my face protection and respect
And I regretted every time I lost my temper
Or didn't pay for the coffee
Or let them shoot the horse or murder a dream

I walked through fire 'til I noticed it didn't burn me
And then, I just stood there in it
And wished it still did
I tried to remember what it was like
When everything mattered and was real
Unlike now when everything matters and is real except for me
As I stand in flames
Unable to burn
And I stand in rain
Dry as the desert
And I stand in cold
Perfectly warm
The sun always shining
Even when
Especially when it's midnight
And there is nothing but darkness
And the whites of your eyes
Reminding to write the poem
To deliver the message
The one that needs to be delivered to you
And then back again
As God talks to himself
Communicates with himself
And showers us with praise
As we lay dying in our inability to surrender
The masters have all been this way before
Though there have been few
They have all burned without burning
Until they were ash
Until they were no more than dust in your eye
Carried by some far off wind
Into your blossoming vision

My broom keeps sweeping every
floor. My floor keeps rising beyond
the sky. My sky keeps sinking
below the ground. This world keeps
blooming.

PEOPLE

People
Almost all of them
Ok
All of them
Walk around with crippled personalities
They have nooses dangling them over flames
And they squirm and choke
In a glance or a cough or the way they say their name or shake
your hand when introduced
People walk around
Afraid of their shadows and their light
Wanting to believe
In something
When doubting everything
Turning each other upside down
In spite and fear
And love is the evil, which locks us together
Looking through ourselves, washed up on oil soaked shores
Under a black sun and demon God

FOR A LITTLE PEACE OF MIND

I wanted you simply to be more forgiving
To be more compassionate
To have more empathy
Even towards someone's unforgivable act

The mad pulse of our culture towards two minutes of hate
It's our own reflection we spit on
It's our own sin we rail against
It's our own self we deem unlovable
And unforgivable

I wanted you simply to flow with love
In the voice of prayer
To take this man at the height of vulnerability
And do the truly generous and revolutionary thing
And forgive
(Yourself through him and his own black heart)
Awaken the voice of compassion
And rise like a phoenix out of his ash
Help his heart heal
Through yours
And the invisible spirit that binds us all

Plus you can trust
That if everyone's going one way
The other way is the way forward

So say a prayer for the one you hate and invariably you pray
for your own peace of mind

And John Lennon would give you everything he's got

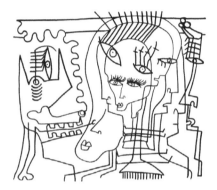

Out here rehearsing. Gone missing.
Saturdays and vandalism. Spray paint
your children on the wall. Lift off and
laugh when the vagrants call.

ALL THE OLD HEROES

Come over old stranger, let go of your dagger
You stagger and then you are saved
To wander in danger, a babe in the manger
Forgetting mistakes that you've made
Eyes like mine blinking
And endlessly drinking
Letting the war lords inside
Falling like mice into fires of ice
In death we find places to hide

All the old heroes are like children to me now
As I come to burn your shame away
Without knowing exactly how

All the old heroes, young babies without mothers
Left to die on apocalyptic streets
And where are these words from who spoke them before?
Coming down like flashes of heat
I'm never frightened, for death I still welcome
Death I have seen you before
I gave you my keys, my windows, my creeds
But soon I will give you much more

All the old heroes are like children to me now
As I come to burn your shame away
Without knowing exactly how

Love is a fix, a suicide wrist
Blood with an unending flow
To purify lands and soak in the sands
Of places that we'll never go

Jesus come calling
We'll be here and falling
Praying for your hand to show
Catch us in mercy, drink us when thirsty
Each of us falling like snow

All the old heroes are like children to me now
As I come to burn your shame away
Without knowing exactly how

Each one a cathedral
The last junkie needle
Stained glass from blood that is old
And in that cathedral, with the angels of nighttime
Pained in a window so cold
They see through your victims your painful musicians
Playing the saddest of songs
But nobody singing, just a ghost without dreaming
A voice that could right all the wrongs

All the old heroes are like children to me now
As I come to burn your shame away
Without knowing exactly how

Goodbye, sweet diamond
The sky in the North wind is falling on lepers and snakes
Hello, young mercy, both blessed and thirsty
For solutions to so many mistakes
Without your lover, your tired wonder
The south rain threatens to pour
On skulls like crashing and sunlight basking
Ignoring the strongest of calls
You cannot save them without their consent

Your voice of mercy to them I have sent
You spoke through me
You, a good man
Grew up to listen and give me your hand
Your voice of mercy so strong and so true
It comes out in cascades without residue
Of darkness or lies or doubt or untruth
It's pure like the wind, the rain, and the youth

All the old heroes are like children to you now
As you go to burn their shame away
Without knowing exactly how
All the old heroes are like children to you now
As you go to burn their shame away

Let the mouse in my house roam
free, and if I come back a zombie, my
arms out haunting you, don't let me
in, but give me a glass of lemonade.

THERE ARE DAYS

There are days which blur into nights,
And nights which blur into days.
The city pushes you into its vacuum.
The city puppets you around stabbing corners,
Over sewers of gold and avenues of blood
Send you swimming up through loneliness
A vagabond. Looking for the company of an angel.

IT TAKES A LOT OF TIME TO LIVE IN THE MOMENT

It takes a lot of time to live in the moment
To become a thing of no thing
To bleed into emptiness
And be sucked up into the cosmos
To reverse aging
And be born again into the arms
Of mother sucking at life
And infinitely charged
It takes a lot of time to live in the moment
To believe without belief
To suffer without grief
To steal the riches without being a thief
By taking it all
The construct
The identity
The ego
And lighting it up with fluid and a Bic
And as it burns
Kick it all
Into the center of the sun
Blow out the sun
The moment
Where dark is light
And blindness sight
Where wrong is right
And day is night
And there is no more me, or you, or time
Or future
Or skin
Or bones
Just the evil low-end buzz consciousness fuzz

Blossoming rose to the nose of eternity eternal
Sucking all the fire from the old sun
And lighting up the new one
For the generations to come
Who have so much time to live in the moment

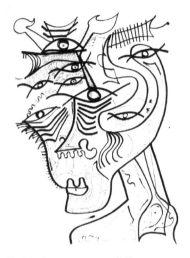

Behind my eyes are different eyes
and behind them even more eyes
which look into the eyes of no
eyes and see nothing but eyes.

MAYBE I'M THROUGH

Maybe I'm through
Getting out of bed
Maybe the waterfall
Just fills up my head
Maybe I'm drowning
Lying next to you
The ghost of no one
Nobody true
The empty space
The river of blood
The lie that dances
Unburdened by love
The noose that hangs
Where little kids play
The kiss of Satan
Where the holiest pray
Maybe I'm through
Looking through glass
I just want touch
And the end of the past
No more future
Just this moment now
Bleeding eternal
In the heat of my brow
Where thoughts just scatter
And tumble and join
As my fate comes landing
As I've tossed like a coin

RESOLUTIONS

(Resolutions
To be naked more
To be more naked
And sure
To trust that
I am God
And perfection is mine
For the price of belief
To forgive
All of them
But mostly myself
My sins)

Like Michael Angelo chipping away at David
Working through karma
To achieve perfection
If not in this life, then the next
To eat chocolate on the roof as dawn strikes through my dreams
Sending shivers over bridges
From Brooklyn to the city (it screams)
Up the Empire State Building and erupting from the tip
Spitting up galaxies and oceans and stars into the sky
As the atmosphere whirls it around 'til the Gods make shapes and
giant beings
Protect us from on high
To be the warrior I have been (or wanted)
But more
And for all time (sometimes hunted)
Sturdy in the stomach
To think of loving others
As I walk by strangers at dusk

To think of the well-being of others
As the singers sing to us and busk
I throw myself in their cases and travel with them on trains
To this and many more places
To be unafraid (in chains)
To love God without shame
To give as is my birthright and purpose
To be true to the depth and beauty of what and who I am
(a heart in surplus)
Though its threat may bring the ridicule of others
It will help many more
Inspire (them like brothers)
To see the same in themselves
Inspire them to inspire me (sister lovers)
And believe you have a very real purpose to fulfill
And it is beyond
Your ideas (or will)
It is beyond your mind's capacity
But you feel it and you know
Who and what you are (a light within the flow)
And what and who you are here to be (God can only know)
Sitting squarely in the middle of this dream
as they all do a dance for you
In the silence of your heart
Between beats
Where new universes get born

I left her there years ago, and I left me
too. Since then I've been engraving
my name in the sky as my flesh falls
away in the wind.

WEDDING DANCE

We did a dance
In a giant dumpster
Just before dawn
I knew there would be gifts in there
How did you know?
God told me
Were you afraid?
No
I am a ninja
We did a dance
She was in first
Pulling the bags away
Fearless and uncontained
Slightly drunk and full of sacred light
I kept checking for cops
None would come
She couldn't do it by herself
A few great little pieces were already liberated
But our work was much deeper than we even knew
Two giant boards
Full of nails and broken pieces of wood
Covered in trash and attached to long metal tails
But it was important to liberate this stuff, and she and I knew why
After equal measures of negotiation and force we were by my
door with the treasure made of trash
At one point she left her bag and notebook behind
Helping me carry the piece called "Donkey Kong" to the door
Everything's deliberate
Everything's liberated
I noted her generosity
Not to her, but to myself

And I thought her things are left there for protection
They
In a way
Will see us through
Once in the long gray hallway
We carried these large pieces full of violence and beauty
We laughed at the insanity of it all
I hit the elevator button several times
But to no avail
Let's carry this stuff up
Ding dong diamond Donkey Kong
Everything, and I mean everything, happens for a reason
These pieces are gonna make us earn their arrival,
And this is how I want it to be.
We begin negotiating this thing up the stairs
A big heavy board full of nails
And an image at the front coming into focus
Donkey Kong
I know who he is
And I know who she is
And I realize that as we walk, lift, beg, crawl, slide, hoist, toss,
levitate, and ninja this thing up the stairs, we are doing so much
more than meets the eye.
For in our partnership to liberate this wood of violence and help
me focus the image of my shadow, I have my muse
negotiating this thing up the stairs.
Slightly tipsy, full of blue-green electric light, having been
swallowed by the night and spit life diamond dust back onto me,
I realize in fact we are doing a wedding dance
And showing each other what it would be like
to relate to each other across a lifetime.
At every turn and in every moment, the potential to be stabbed,
to lose an eye,

to have a hand in the other person's wounding, looms large
She kept saying it's effortless
I had on four or five coats
My face covered in charcoal
My hands like a beautiful red black were in green knit gloves
I had been painting for days and days with little break or no break
She had been at a bar telling somebody she didn't like their music
Because they asked her what she thought,
and because she would rather be painful than a liar
I was sweating all over the place and definitely more of the guide
As I am a fully realized ninja
And as I am the man
Certain principles apply
Not to mention the fact that we were inviting Donkey Kong
into the home
And when you attempt something as large and in charge as that
You must approach the situation with great care and dignity,
You must have prepared the place,
You must know exactly where he will go,
And you must know that once he is inside with you,
Things will never be the same.
You will be whole
And the power that you are no longer afraid of will come flooding
into you directly from the moon, by way of dumpster,
by way of muse, by way of wife, by way of nails which never
broke our flesh through the front door
Five trips up and down those stairs
A wedding dance
Made of nails
Rotting wood
Aluminum tails
Rodent spirits
Laughter

Drunk rain from the light in her eyes
And a smile that goes way beyond generous
This is the story of love

YOU KNOW NOTHING WILL BRING IT/HER BACK

You know nothing will bring it/her back
You will forever be marked
And lonely on a savage planet
When you escape
You disappear
Your ego was built for this
You destroy yourself in the spotlight
Become unglued in the rain
A fading carbon copy of yourself
You bleed as you walk away
Purple ink running behind you
A river
A tiny river
Flowing into a drain
Dripping into the mouth of the beast below
You
Your spirit
You become him
And you lift out of the darkness
Your imaginary life
Your imaginary selves
All running for cover
All being found out
And let down
And tossed into flames
Lives dissected and lost
Lives that never existed
As we all
Have never existed
We are dreams dreaming dreams of loneliness and despair
We mark ourselves and go swimming up rivers of blood

To the empty promise of salvation
But we want it for who we are not
We will never know anything but striving
And survival
I overshot the mark
Forgive me and take me back
I should've been cured long ago
He only now
Is sending angels for me
And I'm not sure it's a good sign
He knows I will fall
He knows I need help through the storm
He's showing me I'm down by sending help
It's not a good sign
I've got one more chance
And I think it's all any of us have

SHE RAN INTO THE STORE

She ran into the store
I waited in the car
The song we just recorded was playing
I began to weep
Nothing could contain my gratitude for this moment
This life
I felt absolved
Saved even
I asked without asking for forgiveness
I was granted without being granted absolution
I was free
A glimpse
An eternal glimpse
Of life outside the human window
The pathways of my sickness
Revealed and relieved
Childish ignorance
Nothing more menacing than that
Just unconsciousness moving to its own will unchecked
Feeding from and being fed to those around
But then the beauty of the song
The love of the people contained therein
The gratitude for a life that has led to this moment and opportunity
A life that has been very painful
But only as a frame for the Godhead center
Like an infinite rose made of consciousness and light breaking
open in slow motion with atom bomb insight into the hearts
and souls of man planted and contained and cared for and
embraced in his heart
And yes I felt or saw or felt/saw his heart
And so I wept

And she ran out of the store
Full of love and generosity
And then she started driving but then noticed my tears
And pulled over
And with her hand
Gently reached over
And wiped them away

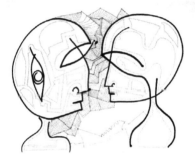

We fell like apples, one rotten, one
fresh. I gotta turn my back on you, I
said - you pretended to understand and
disappeared (or so I thought).

WILLIAMSBURG

I still can't ride through Williamsburg
Without looking for her there,
Every woman with falling eyes
And darkness in her hair.
I see someone she might be,
But I am still not sure.
I stare at the arm, waist and hips
And remember what was pure,
But when she finally turns around
I know that it's not her,
She is someplace faraway
Not this caricature.
The wicked things that lost minds spit,
The wicked things they say
Which keep a heart in wounding hunts
And booby-traps which prey.
On tired souls my weary eyes
Keep looking but still can't see
Her beauty or her touch,
Or the way we used to be.
I still can't walk through Williamsburg,
I have to leave this place
To go somewhere she'll never be
A ghost without a face.
And practice my amnesia,
Practice letting go.
Cast her in forgotten lands
Where all is buried low.
And I can't sleep in Williamsburg
For there she'll steal my dreams,
And haunt me like the one who's damned

And forgotten when he screams.
Love is just a torture now,
This love I wish would die.
I tried to kill it long ago
But forgot the reason why,
Until now here in Williamsburg
Where I see her all around,
Behind each passing stranger,
And in the cracks along the ground.
I see her in the wild sky
Of which I can't escape,
I see her in the empty glass,
In each fermented grape.
I see her in the couples lost,
I see her with some man,
Though I know she'll never love again
The way she knows we can.
But I still can't be in Williamsburg
It's just too lonely here.
And though I was her master
I am mastered now by fear.
As strangers ask me for the train
I point them to the show,
Though I am lost and hollowed out
The need still letting go.

SHE IS STILL A LITTLE GIRL

She is still a little girl
Even though she's almost thirty
We held hands on the park bench
As her friend gathered caterpillars that fell
And put them back on the tree
Cops busted a bum trying to sleep
And we were next
Holding hands
She wore a wedding ring but said they were separated
Said he abused her, and she wanted to move on
To move to NYC
I looked into her big blue eyes
And fell into them
Went swimming in their oceans
Fed my soul into their cosmos
Floated in her outer space thoughts
As her friend picked up caterpillars
She told me about her mother
A right-wing abusive music teacher
And her Native American hippie father
They had split years ago, and she was left with her mother
going from man to man and state to state
The caterpillars will crawl back up the tree and either make
cocoons or fall back to the asphalt and be squashed by cop cars
Bums and basketballs
We were walking back to my bike, it was near dawn and I
had to ride home
I was in love
Though maybe just shallow love
Still love is love
To grown ups sloshing around in a kiddie pool

The whole world is burning up
Her friend the caterpillar lady is mad at us for holding hands
Never trust a hippie
They only espouse those ideals because they are so detached
from them
Hell, I try to detach from them but they ooze out of me like
sweat in a fever dream
I say the opposite of what I think
I kiss her
The child woman wife widow and they get into the cab
The caterpillars are falling again
I get on my bike and flip on the blinking lights
Avoiding drunks and cars and women with bad haircuts
and attitudes
I wish I knew my way home but I only know where I live
A falling caterpillar, riding my bike over the bridge

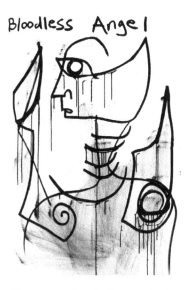

Can you make a balloon out of
rose petals, fill it with helium, and
tie your heart to it, and set it free?

BE CAREFUL OF WITCHES THAT SAY
THEY SPEAK FOR GOD

Be careful of witches that say they speak for God
They come to me
All the time
With messages
Things I'm supposed to do
Things I'm not supposed to
Messages from somewhere else
Not them
Never them
Not their words
People the spirit speaks
Through
They come to
More often than you would think or that seems sane
I attract them
A witch magnet
They have messages
They have insight
They have miracles to bestow
But I feel like shit when they leave
They fill my head with noise
And pretend it comes from somewhere
Other than their own unchecked pain
Things are usually more simple than supernatural
And really the supernatural is quite simple
Things move through stations of love and pain
And how you feel is the best gauge to indicate from where
somebody comes
If when someone leaves, you feel lousy
Then they've dumped pain on your head

If when someone leaves, you feel amazing
Then they've loved the hell out of you
No miracles please
Just give it to me straight
Be real
Take your witchcraft to the guru next door
I'm a psychedelic hillbilly
And I'm close to God and I know it
And you are, too, if you want it
Simple

FOREIGN GIRLS

Seems like all of New York is out today
Tompkins Square Park
A guitarist plays for himself and some pigeons on a green bench
Blending with children's voices dancing in a playground
And muffled adults addressing concerns ... phones evil glaze
People read and dream and throw paper airplanes
In the heat and the haze
As birds watch people twist
And act all strange
All of New York is out today
Tired of being locked in from the winter which just dragged on
Now foreign girls sit next to me
Chatting and smoking
And giggling
They've trapped me
By their beauty
And yet I don't have the energy to start a conversation
I smell their smoke and perfume
And don't know what to say
Other than hello
But instead I sit in silence and mystery
Typing these words into this little machine

Foreign girls
In New York
Sit and smoke
Smoke and talk
Looking for
Dudes and lust
Looking for

A cherry bust
Foreign girls
With speedy tongue
Old enough
But still too young
Sit in daze
Summer glow
By the dude
They want to know

Foreign girls
Plan to drink
Musica and
Lust won't think
Foreign girls
With ripped jeans
They've read about
New York scenes
Foreign girls
Sit and smoke
Perfume kiss
Could make you choke
Show their legs
And glance around
Looking for a thrill
Downtown

Foreign girls
Young and old
Foreign girls
Bought and sold
Foreign girls
Hot and cold

Foreign girls
Made of gold

Everybody loves some
Foreign girls
Everybody wants some
Foreign girls
Everybody hates foreign girls
Foreign girls
Foreign girls
Foreign girls
Foreign girls

Right when I finished the lyrics
The foreign girls got up and left me
I thought for second about reading it to them
But I changed my mind
I watched them walk away
Like angels who brought me a song
And then as if all at once the foreign girls
Were gone

LA STREET SEXY CITY HOLLYWOOD PUPPETS AND SHOW BIZ STARLETS

LA street sexy city Hollywood puppets and show biz starlets breaking hang-ups on countdowns and top ten lists. Plagued by lionhearted zebra dreams of the apocalypse. I bang on drums silently in my backseat confession to no one in particular. The sun a square of itself. Something burning. Multiply universe. Different version of different potentials of you conflicting in dreams walking through fabulous Hollywood parties both naked and invisible. And it's true you don't trust, but that's hardly a curse. However, it's also true you invent your own world. And you let people into your universe by the words and pictures you hang out there on phantom walls and earth shattering apology music. Redemption times ten. How come you never let on who you were? Yeah it's safer to just shit in your nest and eat granola bars and drink stale/burnt coffee. But really. Why not be as powerful as you are? Why not throw your balls across oblivion's table like dice from beyond as you wager your soul? You either go up in flames as a messiah of freedom, or you die homeless babbling to yourself on some street in New Orleans. Let the taillights guide you. Let the monkey on your back make you his slave. And serve the sick and greedy as if they are your superior as you swallow their sickness and the sickness of the world and watch new moons rust as flowers grow out of your eyes.

In life there is this opportunity to know
the ultimate, but there is a fixed amount
of time and a mountain of pain to face and
surpass.

YER ONLY JOB

Yer only job
Is to be free
Free to live
Inside a tree
Free to see
The way you see
If it's strange
Then let it be

Yer only job
Is to be free
Free to laugh
Free to sing
Free to think
You might be king
Or you might fly
Or swim the sea
You have it all
When you are free

But freedom
Puts the fear in some
And they will tell you
Not to run
And not to dream
All you see
Inside the open
World of free

For freedom follows
No command
It has no feet
No arm or hand

It has no language
It has no rhyme
It has no clock
No goal or time

For freedom is
Its own reward
Its own protection
Without a sword
Without a fight
Freedom stands
Holding on
With phantom hands
To yer heart
Of the sky
Winter lips
Mountains cry

Freedom holds
The world above
The reach of death
The reach of love

Freedom is
Its own reward
Distorted power
Singing chord
Freedom lifts
The stars in space
Freedom is
An angel's face
The planets bouncing
Rubber balls
Freedom bouncing

Off yer walls
You catch and throw
And catch some more
Freedom opens
Every door

Just remember
To be free
And you will be
The same as me
And I will be
The same as you
Sniffing flowers
Freedom glue
Stuck to stars
Which shoot through skies
The twinkle twinkle
In yer eyes
The bed of love
On which you sleep
The day of hope
The one you greet
The night of dreams
Both big and small
The call you hear
Down freedom's hall

Come home now
For home you're in
One day gone
The next begin
It's a circle
Like wheels which ride
The waves of oceans

Freedom tide
Welcome home
You never left
Maybe lost
Freedom theft
But you got found
Freedom bee
Buzzing for
Eternity
And freedom is
The light you see
Enlightened soul
Turning key
Others see
And may wake up
Inspiration
Freedom cup
Drink the nectar
Of the soul

Freedom is
An endless hole
Which opens up
In the sky
It's a circle
You and I
We are one
We are free
I am you
And you are me

Yes we are one
When we are free
For I am you
And you are me

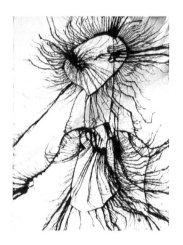

Sometimes the water must be
cold, or the person will stay
asleep. Sometimes love needs
be harsh. Its foes are worthy.
Unconsciousness/fear.

SOMETIME IN NEW ORLEANS

Along the edge of the Mississippi
A thousand hearts bled into this
My heart looking for something to execute
Beats in the Mississippi
Underneath up against its current
My heart so alive submerged in the dark
The airless dark the flow of my blood so violent and berserk
Who could hold me here?
Who could hold me down?
Sitting on the edge of the Mississippi
River of slaves
River of bones
I have been down here across generations
Lifetimes ago
I was sold amongst the thieves
I don't ignore the cries
I hear them
I am conscious along the Mississippi
I hear the footsteps of ghosts
I hear them scream behind me
I see their boats sink
As I am so very alive
She draws me to her breath
She whispers with her voice
Her comfort is all I want, all I need
Alone on Saturday night
Me and the Mississippi
Two rivers flowing together
Flowing internal
A river of darkness

A river of light
Blend as one in my mind eternal
Forever together against the impossible ends we face
Our lunatic charm
She can never claim me
Nor I her
We flow together eternal
We flow together as one
I am the Mississippi
She has made me her own

HEADING TO THE END OF THE NEW WORLD

Heading to the end of the new world
Heading to the beginning of the old revolution
No one to stick it to
Nothing to give or prove
Just idiot glee
And a kind of heart attack stance
Nothing here is true
Nothing here is different
Just the dawn and the driver and the plane and the take off
Who is this new audience?
Who is this witness? This mourning?
Whose confusion is this so easily disregarded?
So easily disposed of?
This device holds no music
This device
Needs words
Needs soul
Who am I to not believe in myself?
Think of the lunacy of it
Who is this small parasite in my head?
Chewing north
Swallowing the soul of a king
Swallowing the kingdom with an impoverished apathy
Which salutes no one and hides in the spade and the meadow and
the begging and the drunk
Spread your legs, dear lady, and let me be born
Spread your legs, I want to talk to God
Spread your legs and allow me to see from where I come
Spread your legs and allow me to rewind this life
Allow me to obliterate this ghost
Or send him back up through you to the kingdom

Spread your legs, dear lady, and let me dream
You are the connection between heaven and earth
You are man's passage to eternity
You are man's fortress and his destruction
I am ready to be destroyed in your light
I am ready for the lepers to dissipate and dissolve
I am ready for freedom, which never evaporates
I am ready for a freedom in love

THIS PLACE

This place
It drives you inside
Drives you internal
Maybe if you're lucky, eternal
But never mind that
I overate
This place
High school reunion
So many ghosts in a bar doing shots
Strangers or the only ones who know you
Life goes by in blazes and this place
Sits quiet like the stomach of God
You are inside being digested
Your emotions flooding
This place
It's dark and quiet and there is nothing to do or no one to beg
Or nowhere to drive
And this place just whispers hollow dreams
About the march of time
Running over everyone
Lucky to have made it to adulthood
We all have baggage to carry
You're not the only one
And this place
It's a meditation on escape
And you are its son
The golden beggar
The beginner, the old beginner
Full of birds and battles
Solutions and syringes
Maybe you failed someone or maybe you are too hard on yourself

Maybe people are impossible to save
And maybe your heart is a desert
This place gave you all this life and here you just spin out of control
You've always been lonely
And you've always needed the night to release
But it never has
And it never will

Tunes which crawl or fall through cracks of time. Blood melodies bleeding in keys unknown. 'Cept for ghosts who look at you wandering and laugh.

RIDE THROUGH THE CITY

Ride through the city
Brooklyn at night
The moon shows her teeth
On my neck she will bite
I am her child
Her child of scorn
Eyes/wheels in motion
Dreams being born
Over lost bridges
The blind getting sight
Boondocks and ridges
And ferries that fight
For pathways on water
Both black, gray, and white
Nighttime in color
Then colorless height
You fall, I follow
This town bending down
Both deep and then shallow
In waters we drown
Moon turns to shadow
Then sunlight beyond
The tears of the widow
Her love moving on
To worlds after this one
To worlds no one knows
Where everything echoes
And even death grows
Everything backwards
Like nudists in clothes
To worlds she can dream on

With sky walking toes
Her walk through the clouds
Like a child of flight
As this world rebounds
And the new world is bright
Ride through the city
Under the trees
Streetlamps and strangers
And glances which freeze
Bugs storming windows
Dark eyes look out
Fear taking leaps
And quiet moans shout
Who have you been?
Where did you go?
Were you with Hector,
Sidney or Joe?
Mission accomplished
Or buried in snow
Was your life empty,
Or full with the flow?
Did you ignite
The source of the hole?
Did her legs open?
Was her heart coal?
To turn into diamonds
Were you reborn?
Was truth a question,
Or just merely worn?
Like designs on a t-shirt
A design you could fold
When you opened your mouth
For lies being told

Have you shown mercy,
In deaths hollow morn?
Or were you a ransom
In the hostage of porn?
Cold looking out
Deceit looking in
When you were finished
Did you begin?
Did you wear wires?
Were you a rat?
Dead in the alley
Alive like a cat
Walk past a stranger
Black for their luck
Make sure they see you
Then jump on a truck
Become a cartoon
Like Donald Duck
And if they don't hurt you
Help them to suck
The light from the darkness
Through wonder and joy
Your heart in its starkness
An elegant toy
A wind up for Buddha, for Krishna,
For Christ
A wind up for thieves
Still drunk from the heist
Your skin
Burned and broken
Both man and machine
The whole world is open
And lost in your spleen

Take out the toxins
And with them make gold
Be unafraid and in new worlds
Be bold
Be like Muhammad
Be like the rain
Put all your dreams
On a broken down train
Then walk away
And dream them again
Lift up the day
To the night's lonely spin
Bite off a leg
Whirl her around
The moon and you play
With the sun
Falling down
Ride through the city
Lunch with a priest
How long will you starve
In front of the feast?
When will you carve
Yourself out a piece
And feed from your place in the world?
(When will you carve
Yourself out of peace
And feed your whole self to the world?)

EAST VILLAGE MYSTIC

I spend days in the confused room of the spirit.
I eat almonds off my stomach.
Voices rise up
And plead their case
Before judges who shrivel,
And die,
And become dust,
And blow
Into the hollow eyes of creation
Where they are swallowed
And forgotten,
Redeemed and forgiven.
I meditate in the bath
And tap on my forehead
And my chest reciting prayers,
As I can feel
Myself embraced and heard
If only by phantoms
Or illness
In the mind, and it is better than smoking crack in Times
Square.
Marked up by amnesia
And ink and mushrooms
And an insatiable greed for love,
A hole in me,
The size of the world.
Wound up like a metal toy
From the fifties, rusted
And dumb and betrayed by gravity.
I return to the rooms of the spirit
To listen to them

Speak,
To hear them share
The destruction and resurrection
Of their lives.
Even as they speak
From beyond this life,
Even as they crowd
Around old doors smoking,
Even as they are mostly
Liars and thieves,
They are also mystics
And boogie men
And hookers and saints.
Mostly I just ride,
But
As I leap
Into freedom,
Looking up and asking him to show me
What it is I am here to see,
Beyond infinity swallowing itself into a body of a man
Driven by love,
To reach love,
To give love,
To get love,
To defeat love,
Or else just to see
How love can mean freedom
And always be free.

On my way. Missions kissing the toes of destiny. Holding hands with redemption. Biting love on the neck. Welcoming the new age. Forgiving.

THOUGHTS ON ART

Thoughts on art
Nothing should be wasted.
(It's all waste)
(It's all wasted)
Hunger is good.
Hunger is profound,
But it can destroy.
It's good to be hungry
But not starving.
When things come from your animal survival,
They hold more weight.
They are necessary.
All the best things are necessary.
Nothing is necessary
To survive as an artist.
You have to be willing to surrender it all
And fall off the face of the planet
Into the cosmos,
Into the face of the clock spinning backwards.
You have to be willing to live in a garage
Or along train tracks or in a mansion or a submarine.
You have to be charged with infinity but confused about everything.
You have to be a clown and a king.
These are thoughts on art,
Though I have no thoughts or art,
Just a will to start and bleed,
And maybe that's all it takes.
A touch of nihilism goes a long way.
It's good, too,
To be a little bit suicidal,
Not enough to actually do it

But enough to not care what happens to you,
For you have to throw yourself
To the wolves
And they will show no mercy
As they rip your throat out.
It's good to be able to smile
As if it's what you expected the entire time.
But then, too,
You have to trust
As if a child,
As if your prayers will be answered, as if the horrible things
are still somewhere out there and in the distance.
You have to feel protected (at least some of the time)
And still aiming to value life enough to breath more value
into life.
You have to be beautiful when you are ugly
And ugly when you are beautiful.
And amongst the cacophony of chaos,
Amongst the city screaming its indifference like a train
through your skull,
Amongst the billions of galaxies beyond this one and the
billions more beyond,
As the universe is expanding
Into what?
You have to believe
Somebody hears your whisper
Lying in the dark alone
Waiting for sleep to come.

I MISS THE ZOO

I miss the drunk
I miss the fiend
I miss the simplicity of addiction
And the scene
I miss wandering aimlessly
In half dead sewers with rats for eyes
Chewing on forgiveness
And the will to apologize
I miss the return of no return
As I burn in avalanches
Of white snow and yellow cocaine
I miss talking to brick walls
While following the grain
And human dolls as I plagiarize myself like a dummy
Stuffed with counterfeit money
For Cairo and black honey
I miss illusions begging to be chased
Even as they disappear into me (erased)
Until there is no one or nothing but the chase
And a powdery ghost with no face
(Or faith)
And the woman of my dreams disappearing without grace
I miss evolving into a cloud
Of blue marijuana blown from the lips
Of hookers and pimps
As they smack each other down
In alleys for the dammed but mighty
With no one but the weak around
And the beautiful unsightly
I miss numb Neanderthals marching
In rows of living dead

From my wisdom teeth to Spain and back again (in my head)
I miss salvation in syringes and angels of mercy
In blooms of smoke numbing rain
Which drinks when thirsty
I miss glasses full of spirits
Who without tongues speak to me of Napoleon's wild nights
I miss staying up for days and becoming a psychic pretzel
Flying kites
Chewed on by a Zulu heading with toads to Mars
A mysterious prison
And one without bars
Just strange candy and shooting stars
I miss waking in the arms of strangers
Like puppies just born in the pound to a dead mother with eyes
sealed shut
Looking for a tit to suck
And other dangers
When the night before laughter was our only pursuit
Even as knives carved up our backs
And demons sat like Buddhas eating fruit
Meditating on hate forever in our minds
I miss exposing even my bones
And the need that rewinds
Even my burning home
Even my gutted inner child
Even my dead grandfather
Beneath the ground that's wild
Even my criminal family
Even my weed wacker thoughts
Whipping a thin plastic string
To cut the ears off others
As I sing
I miss van Gogh's revenge

I miss his nightly binge
I miss spiders surrounding my bed
And lifting me as if an effigy or
Dead
King or a prophet of doom
A Jesus for the apocalypse
Wearing dirt like perfume
Or a mother for Satan
Or ghost for all the children of abuse
And taking me into the fire
Watching me burn
Like a goose
As they sing
In spider voices
There goes creation there goes the moon
There goes the butterfly
Wanting cocoon
I miss being a bloom
And a goon
I miss waking up too soon in the afternoon
A doctor of regret
Hanging onto guitar strings in tune
And hanging by a belt
Wrapped around some pipe
To nowhere and felt
My lips too wrapped around
What appears to be stained glass
As religious figures dress like
Rocks with class burn into gas
To the center of my brain
The euphoria of dying and being born all at once
While wearing the hat that reads "dunce"

Joseph Arthur is a poet, artist, and musician from the
Midwest. He has worked with Peter Gabriel, Michael Stipe,
Ben Harper and Dhani Harrison, and most recently with
Jeff Ament of Pearl Jam in the band RNDM. His latest studio
album is *The Ballad of Boogie Christ*. He has exhibited
his artwork in Paris, Los Angeles, Montreal and most recently
at Able Fine Art in New York. This is his first book of poems
published with EM Press.